30382065R00057

Made in the USA
Lexington, KY
09 February 2019